IONS

Birthday

FIONA MACMATH
Illustrated by Sara Silcock

Hunt & Thorpe

A Delight

"Poor Eeyore is in a Very Sad Condition," said Pooh, "because it's his birthday, and nobody has taken any notice of it, and he's very Gloomy."

AA MILNE: *WINNIE THE POOH*

What happens to our birthdays when we grow up? A child's birthday is fun: candy and balloons, cakes and candles – everything is greeted with delight. The giver of each gift is more than rewarded by the child's surprise and happiness.

Older but not Wiser

You don't have to look hard to see that adults aren't so good at birthdays. The problem is that as we grow older, our attitude to birthdays fails to mature. It is fine to use birthdays as a way to escape back to our childhood, but there is a much greater richness available to us if we can find it. A child's joy is pure and uncomplicated. As we learn more about the world, our joy is tempered by the experience of sadder things. All this should make a birthday more precious. But instead we find worries and anxieties surfacing.

The Thought that Counts

What's the most exciting thing about birthdays? Receiving presents! You've reached a high state of spiritual detachment if you can answer anything different. But as we grow up, we begin to appreciate what lies behind the present.

You are given a sweater. The person who gave it likes you, perhaps loves you. No matter if it's a funny shape and the wrong size. The love behind it is probably a funny shape and the wrong size, too.But it says that there's one person here who is pleased that you're around on the planet; so pleased, that they've remembered your birthday and given you something to help you celebrate it. Maybe you didn't even have to remind them.

'I Like You'

We tend not to go up to our friends and tell them to their faces how much we like them and are pleased to have them around. It's a shame, because the world would be a better place if we did. So sending a birthday present – maybe even just a card – is the nearest we usually get. Don't underestimate it.

Of course there is much that is conventional about the way we celebrate birthdays, and you may feel that many of your presents have been given out of duty, not love. Alright then, do something about it. Nurture the relationship in the year ahead of you and put genuine affection back into it. And avoid the same trap yourself when it comes to giving presents to others.

Birthday Tears

Do you number your birthdays with thankfulness? Do you overlook the faults of your friends? Do you become gentler and better as old age approaches?

HORACE: *EPISTLES*

At children's parties there comes the moment when the excitement burns itself out – rather like the bursting of a balloon. The child looks around at the jumble of wrapping paper and asks: "Is that it?" Then you have to be on the lookout for tears.

This feeling doesn't go away as we get older. It is uncanny how what should be one of the happiest days of the year should contain some of the most distressing moments for such a lot of people. Many avoid the distress by racing through their birthday and not allowing themselves any time to reflect. Some even 'forget' their birthdays altogether. But still that same question creeps through our defences: "Is that it?"

This time, though, it doesn't apply to the presents or the party arrangements. The occasion is really quite a serious one. We are recollecting the moment of our birth. Our very existence. Life itself is a gift; and we receive it as such, with thanks to the Giver.

A Time to Look Back

It is natural that our thoughts become more sober: "OK, I was given this existence so many years ago. What have I done with it since then?" Centuries ago, it was common for people to use the occasion of their birthdays to consider what they had learned from life up till then. For many of us, the time for this sort of reflection has shifted to New Year's Eve (except for the fact that so many of us have squeezed the thinking time out of that day, too). It's time to shift things back again.

There is quite a knack to looking back, or self-assessment. We're very good at seeing things only in the way we *want* to see them – maybe the only way we can see them.

Be Positive

I sometimes pray not for self–knowledge in general but for just so much self–knowledge at the moment as I can bear and use at the moment; the little daily dose.

C.S.LEWIS: *LETTERS TO MALCOLM*

Some of us, look back and see only *what has happened to us*, and so shirk responsibility for our failings and the things that have gone wrong because of us. Others go to the opposite extreme and see the past in terms of *what they have done*, taking their own actions too much into account and developing a huge sense of guilt. All this is very one-sided. How can we blame others for not seeing the good in our lives if we do not appreciate it ourselves?

A birthday is a good time to concentrate on the positive bits of life so far. Nobody's listening, so no false modesty. Admit to yourself: "Yes, I have been kinder to my children" or "Yes, I have worked harder in my job." There will be other days when you can reflect on the less flattering things.

A Time to Look Forward

Show me, O Lord, my life's end and
the number of my days;
Let me know how fleeting is my life .

PSALM 39, VERSE 4

A birthday is a time for looking in two directions, forward as well as back. It would be foolish to shy away from it: a birthday tells us that we are getting older. After a certain point, our abilities will start to decline and poor health will threaten. And death seems closer. But to fear this is to get caught up in the land–locked view of life and death. There is a better way of seeing things.

Life is more than just existence; more than the passage of time which we notice most on our birthdays. It is a way of being, a power to act, feel, think, love. In the Bible, the word is seldom used in the narrow sense of just being alive. Instead it means becoming part of God's power that shapes and maintains the world.

Life to the Full

For Jesus, life was something tremendously important, which he could see stretching out into eternity. For this reason, he spoke not about bodily death. Rather, he was concerned with those things which killed off areas of a person's life: selfishness, pride, greed, lack of belief.

Whoever hears my word and believes him who sent me has eternal life and will not be condemned; he has crossed over from death to life.
JOHN 5:24

I came that they mayhave life,
and have it to the full.
JOHN **10:10**

A New Life

Grow old along with me!
The best is yet to be,
The last of life, for which the first was made:
Our times are in His hand
Who saith, "A whole I planned,
Youth shows but half; trust God; see all,
nor be afraid!"

ROBERT BROWNING, FROM *RABBI BEN EZRA*

The life we celebrate with each birthday should be a real life, the life we were given at birth that grows richer as we mature. The blossoms of springtime must die to bring forth the sweet apples of autumn.

And for the Christian, the story goes one stage further. The apples fall and decay, releasing the seed buried within, which will in turn begin life afresh – the eternal life which Jesus offers. How ridiculous to mourn the 'loss' of one year when our lives stretch far into the mysteries of heaven.

As you stand at the start of a new year, take hold of this life and rejoice!

First published by Hunt & Thorpe 1991
ISBN 1 85608 071 4

The CIP catalogue record for this book is available from the British Library.

Manufactured in Italy.